# The Trust Vacuum

*How People Rebuild Reality When Institutions Stop Making Sense*

# The Trust Vacuum

*How People Rebuild Reality When Institutions Stop Making Sense*

The Trust Vacuum:
How People Rebuild Reality When Institutions Stop Making Sense

Richard Rawson, Psy.D., MBA

© 2026 Richard Rawson
All rights reserved.

No part of this book may be reproduced, stored, or transmitted in any form or by any means without the prior written permission of the author, except for brief quotations used in reviews or scholarly works.

This book is intended for educational and informational purposes only. It does not constitute professional, legal, or clinical advice.

ISBN: 979-8-9946881-4-4

Published by Rawson Internet Marketing.
United States of America.

# Table of Contents

Chapter 1: When Authority Stops Working . . . . . . . . 1

Chapter 2: Why Skepticism Is Not the End State . . . . . . 7

Chapter 3: The Psychological Need for Coherent Reality . . 13

Chapter 4: From Institutions to Informal Authority . . . . . 19

Chapter 5: How People Decide What's True . . . . . . . . 25

Chapter 6: Identity-Based Credibility . . . . . . . . . . 31

Chapter 7: Subcultures as Trust Infrastructure . . . . . . . 37

Chapter 8: Influencers, Para-Experts, and Private Authorities . 41

Chapter 9: The Moral Authority of "Do Your Own Research?" . 45

Chapter 10: Narrative Authority vs. Institutional Authority . . 49

Chapter 11: Conspiracy As Coherent Reality-Building . . . 53

Chapter 12: Why Conspiracies Persist After Disconfirmation . 57

Chapter 13: Competing Realities and Social Friction . . . . 63

Chapter 14: The Costs and Benefits of Replacement Systems . 67

Chapter 15: What Shared Reality Used To Do . . . . . . . 73

Chapter 16: Reality After Institutions . . . . . . . . . . 77

WHEN AUTHORITY STOPS WORKING

# CHAPTER 1
# When Authority Stops Working

WHEN AUTHORITY STOPS WORKING

# When Authority Stops Working

Institutions can continue to exist long after they stop doing the psychological work people once relied on them to do. Buildings remain. Titles remain. Experts still speak. Reports are still issued. From the outside, it can look like nothing fundamental has changed. But for many people, something has shifted at a deeper level. The institution may still function, yet it no longer organizes reality in the same way.

What is lost is not just confidence in a particular agency, profession, or organization. What erodes is the quiet assumption that there is a shared place to stand when deciding what counts as real, credible, or legitimate. When that assumption weakens, people do not simply become more careful thinkers. They lose a common reference point that once made everyday judgments feel grounded.

This kind of erosion is difficult to see because it does not always show up as open rebellion or explicit rejection. People may still watch the news, go to the doctor, follow laws, or send their children to school. On the surface, participation continues. Underneath, however, the relationship has changed. Authority is no longer taken for granted as something that reliably organizes what people accept as real. It becomes one voice among many, rather than the place where reality is settled.

In earlier periods, institutions did more than provide information or services. They reduced uncertainty. They created shared standards for what counted as evidence, expertise, and normal disagreement. They offered a sense that even when people argued, they were still arguing within the same basic frame. You could disagree about conclusions while still trusting the process that produced them.

When that frame weakens, people are left with a more exposed psychological task. They still have to decide what to believe, who to trust, and how to interpret events. The difference is that there is no longer a widely accepted structure doing that work in the background. What once felt settled now feels provisional. What once felt obvious now feels negotiable.

This does not usually lead to calm neutrality. Sustained uncertainty is uncomfortable. Human beings are not built to live for long in a state where nothing reliably anchors interpretation. Everyday life requires decisions, judgments, and a sense of what matters. When institutions stop providing that scaffolding, people feel the pressure to rebuild it in other ways.

This is not mainly an intellectual problem. It is a practical and emotional one. People need workable maps of reality in order to function. They need ways to decide what to pay attention to, who to listen to, and how to explain what is happening around them. When institutional authority no longer supplies those maps in a convincing way, people do not stop mapping. They start drawing their own.

From the outside, this can look like confusion, irrationality, or stubbornness. From the inside, it often feels like necessity. If the old systems no longer make sense of lived experience, people look for systems that do. They search for explanations that fit what they are seeing, feeling, and encountering in their own lives. The question is no longer simply, "What do the authorities say?" It becomes, "What actually helps me make sense of this?"

This is the point at which the trust vacuum opens. The space left behind by weakened authority does not remain empty. It becomes an active zone where new forms of credibility, explanation, and meaning rush in. The institutional voice is no longer the default place people start. It must compete with many other voices that claim to explain what is really going on.

Once that competition begins, the role of authority changes. It is no longer a background structure that quietly organizes reality. It becomes one narrative among others, one perspective among many, one option among many competing explanations. For people living inside this shift, reality itself begins to feel less shared and more assembled.

This book is not about whether institutions deserve trust. That is a separate question. The focus here is on what happens psychologically and socially when institutions, for whatever reason, stop performing their old role as central organizers of meaning. The deeper issue is not the loss of trust alone. It is the loss of a shared mechanism for deciding what is real, and what fills that space when it disappears.

## The Trust Vacuum

What follows is not a story of people becoming purely skeptical. It is a story of people becoming builders. When authority stops working the way it once did, people do not live in a vacuum for long. They begin constructing replacement systems that can carry the weight that institutions used to carry for them.

WHY SKEPTICISM IS NOT THE END STATE

# CHAPTER 2

# Why Skepticism Is Not The End State

# Why Skepticism Is Not The End State

When people lose trust in traditional authorities, it is often described as a turn toward skepticism. From the outside, it can look like people have simply become more critical, more questioning, or harder to persuade. That description captures something real, but it misses what actually happens over time. Sustained skepticism is not a stable psychological position. It works as a transitional state, not as a place most people can live for long.

Doubt can feel clarifying at first. It can create a sense of independence and relief, especially for people who believe they have been misled or talked down to. Questioning official narratives can feel like taking back control of one's own judgment. For a period, skepticism itself can function as a kind of identity. It separates a person from what they now see as naïve acceptance.

Over time, however, doubt becomes exhausting. Everyday life does not pause while people hold everything in suspension. Decisions still have to be made. Risks still have to be assessed. Explanations still have to be chosen, even if reluctantly. Living in a permanent state of "maybe nothing is true" quickly becomes unworkable. The human mind looks for something more solid to stand on.

This is where skepticism quietly gives way to construction. People begin to replace what they no longer trust with something they can use. They may not describe this as building something new, but that is what it amounts to. They assemble new rules for deciding what makes sense, who seems credible, and which explanations feel plausible enough to live with.

This shift is often invisible to the person experiencing it. From their point of view, they are not abandoning skepticism. They are refining it. They may say they are just being careful, or just following the evidence, or just thinking for themselves. What is happening underneath is that new standards are being adopted. These standards are rarely formal, but they are real. They shape what gets taken seriously and what gets dismissed.

Once this happens, skepticism stops being a neutral filter and becomes part of a larger framework. Certain sources are treated as obviously untrustworthy. Others are treated as more honest, more realistic, or more aligned with lived experience. Over time, patterns form. A person may not be able to list their rules explicitly, but they can feel when something "doesn't add up" or when a story "sounds right."

This is not a failure of reasoning. It is a response to psychological pressure. Human beings need working explanations in order to function. They need ways to decide where to place their attention, what risks to worry about, and how to interpret confusing events. Pure skepticism does not provide that. It only removes old answers. It does not supply new ones.

For many people, skepticism also becomes socially isolating if it remains purely negative. Constantly saying what you do not believe does not create much of a shared world with other people. Over time, most people gravitate toward frameworks that allow them to connect, compare notes, and feel understood. That pull toward shared meaning is strong, even when people are wary of traditional authorities.

As a result, skepticism often evolves into something more structured. People begin to recognize familiar narratives, trusted voices, and recurring explanations. They start to notice which interpretations resonate within their circles and which ones fall flat. Belief systems begin to take shape, even if they are described as open-minded or provisional.

At this point, the language of skepticism can mask what is really happening. A person may continue to say they are just asking questions. At the same time, they may show strong confidence in certain stories, strong distrust of others, and strong emotional reactions when their preferred explanations are challenged. The posture remains skeptical, but the function has changed. A new system is doing the work that institutions once did.

This is why attempts to correct people by appealing to skepticism often fail. From the outside, it looks like someone is being inconsistent. If they are skeptical, why are they so certain about this one explanation. From the inside, it feels coherent. The person is no longer choosing between belief and doubt in the abstract. They are choosing between competing systems that offer different ways to make sense of reality.

In this sense, skepticism is best understood as a bridge, not a destination. It helps people step away from frameworks that no longer feel trustworthy. It rarely sustains them on its own. What follows is usually the slow, often unconscious building of a new structure of credibility, explanation, and belonging.

By the time this process is underway, the question is no longer whether someone is skeptical. The question is which system they are now using to decide what counts as real. The trust vacuum does not stay empty. Skepticism clears space. Something else always moves in to fill it.

# CHAPTER 3
# The Psychological Need for Coherent Reality

## The Psychological Need For Coherent Reality

Human beings do not relate to the world as a collection of isolated facts. They rely on patterns, stories, and shared understandings to make experience feel navigable. Even in ordinary, low-stress situations, people are constantly interpreting what is happening, why it is happening, and what it means for them. These interpretations are not optional. They are part of how the mind keeps life manageable.

A coherent sense of reality reduces cognitive and emotional load. When people can rely on shared frameworks, they do not have to evaluate everything from scratch. They can assume that certain sources are credible, that certain explanations are reasonable, and that certain disagreements fall within acceptable bounds. This does not eliminate uncertainty, but it keeps uncertainty within tolerable limits.

Without this kind of coherence, everyday life becomes more taxing. Small decisions begin to feel heavier. Ordinary news can feel destabilizing. People may find themselves repeatedly revisiting questions that once felt settled. Over time, this creates fatigue. The mind looks for ways to restore a sense of order, even if the new order is imperfect.

Coherence is also closely tied to identity. People do not just want to know what is true. They want to know where they stand in relation to what is true. Shared frameworks help people locate themselves. They provide cues about what kinds of people they are, what values they hold, and what groups they belong to. When those frameworks weaken, identity can feel less anchored.

This is one reason institutional erosion often feels personal, even when it is discussed in abstract terms. When shared standards break down, people lose more than a set of rules. They lose part of the structure that tells them who they are in relation to the world. The task of rebuilding reality is also a task of rebuilding self-understanding.

Coherent reality also supports emotional regulation. When people can interpret events within a stable frame, they can calibrate their reactions. They can decide what deserves strong emotion and what can be taken in stride. They can distinguish between signal and noise. When coherence weakens, emotional responses become harder to pace. Everything can start to feel urgent, threatening, or overwhelming.

In this sense, coherence is not about being right in some abstract, philosophical way. It is about having a reality that is usable. A usable reality allows people to plan, to trust, to disagree without falling apart, and to absorb new information without constantly reworking their entire worldview. When that usability is lost, people feel it quickly, even if they cannot name it.

The psychological pressure to restore coherence is powerful. It does not wait for careful philosophical reflection. It operates at the level of everyday functioning. People look for explanations that reduce confusion, restore a sense of order, and allow them to move forward without feeling constantly off balance.

This is why replacement systems often take hold even when they are incomplete, biased, or internally inconsistent. From the outside, it can be tempting to ask why people would adopt frameworks that seem flawed. From the inside, the comparison is rarely between perfect truth and flawed belief. It is between ongoing disorientation and a story that makes enough sense to live with.

Once a framework provides enough stability, it tends to be defended. Not only because people think it is true, but because it is doing important psychological work. It is helping them feel oriented. It is helping them decide what matters. It is helping them maintain a sense of self in a world that feels less stable.

This does not mean that people consciously choose coherence over accuracy. It means that coherence and accuracy become difficult to separate in lived experience. What feels true is often what feels stabilizing. What feels destabilizing is often treated as suspect. Over time, the line between what feels true and what feels emotionally survivable becomes blurred.

Understanding this need for coherent reality is essential for understanding what fills the trust vacuum. People are not simply choosing ideas. They are choosing ways of organizing experience that allow them to function. Replacement systems succeed not only because of what they claim, but because of how they make life feel more navigable.

In the chapters that follow, this dynamic will appear again and again. New sources of authority, new narratives, and new credibility systems do not spread only because they persuade. They spread because they offer coherence in a world where old frameworks no longer reliably do.

# CHAPTER 4
# From Institutions To Informal Authority

## From Institutions To Informal Authority

When institutional authority weakens, it does not disappear. It relocates. The need for guidance, interpretation, and credibility remains. What changes is where people look to have those needs met. Instead of defaulting to formal organizations, people increasingly turn to individuals, networks, and informal sources that feel more accessible and more responsive to their lived experience.

This shift is often gradual. People may not consciously decide to replace institutions with informal authorities. It happens through small adjustments in attention and trust. A person may start by listening to a podcast host who seems to explain things more clearly than official spokespeople. They may follow a social media account that appears to notice patterns the news does not cover. Over time, these sources begin to carry more weight in shaping how events are interpreted.

Informal authority is often more personal. It is delivered in a voice that sounds human rather than institutional. It includes stories, emotions, and direct reactions. This can create a sense of closeness and understanding that formal communication rarely provides. People feel like someone is speaking to them rather than at them.

Relational proximity plays a large role in this process. When someone feels like they know a source, even in a one-sided way, trust can grow quickly. A familiar voice, a consistent presence, or shared language can create a sense of credibility that does not depend on credentials. The authority comes from perceived alignment, not formal standing.

Networks also begin to matter more. Friends, family members, and online communities become important filters for what information is taken seriously. Recommendations travel through social ties. If people you trust take something seriously, you are more likely to do the same. This social reinforcement can be more powerful than any institutional endorsement.

Over time, informal authorities develop recognizable roles. Some people become known as the one who "really understands what's going on." Others become interpreters who translate complex events into emotionally resonant narratives. Some position themselves as truth-tellers who claim to say what institutions will not. Each role offers a different way of organizing reality.

The appeal of informal authority is not just about content. It is also about style and stance. Informal sources often acknowledge uncertainty, express emotion, and show personal investment. This can make their interpretations feel more honest, even when the factual basis is unclear. The presence of visible human judgment can feel more trustworthy than the impersonal tone of institutional communication.

As this shift continues, people may not feel that they are rejecting institutions outright. They may still consult official sources. The difference is that those sources are no longer primary. They are weighed alongside, or filtered through, informal authorities that feel more aligned with personal experience and group identity.

This reorganization of authority changes how credibility is evaluated. Instead of asking whether a source has formal expertise, people increasingly ask whether a source seems to understand people like them. Trust becomes relational and contextual. It is tied to perceived shared values, shared frustrations, and shared ways of interpreting events.

Once informal authority becomes established, it can be surprisingly durable. A trusted informal source can maintain influence even when they are wrong, because their credibility is based on relationship and identity, not just accuracy. Challenges to their claims can feel like personal attacks rather than neutral corrections.

From the outside, this can look like people choosing charisma over expertise. From the inside, it feels like choosing someone who "gets it" over someone who feels distant or disconnected. The emotional logic makes sense even when the informational logic is shaky.

This does not mean that informal authority is always misguided. In many cases, people turn to it because institutions have failed to address real concerns, communicate clearly, or demonstrate responsiveness. Informal sources can fill genuine gaps. The problem is not that people seek alternatives. The problem is that alternatives become the primary structures for defining reality.

As informal authority grows, the landscape of credibility becomes more fragmented. Different groups follow different voices. Different networks privilege different interpreters. What counts as a trusted explanation in one circle may be dismissed outright in another. Shared reality becomes harder to sustain, not because people have stopped caring about truth, but because they are now anchored to different sources of it.

This chapter describes a structural shift, not a moral failing. People are responding to changes in how authority is experienced. When institutions no longer feel reliable, responsive, or aligned, people do what humans have always done. They turn to sources that feel closer, more understandable, and more attuned to their lives.

What emerges is not the absence of authority, but a patchwork of informal authorities. These new structures carry real psychological weight. They shape what people notice, how they interpret events, and who they believe when stories conflict. The trust vacuum is not empty. It is crowded with new voices, each offering a different way to make sense of the world.

# How People Decide What's True

# CHAPTER 5
# How People Decide What's True

How People Decide What's True

## How People Decide What's True

When shared standards weaken, people do not stop making judgments about reality. They continue to decide what they believe, what they doubt, and what they treat as reliable. The difference is that these decisions become more individualized and less anchored to widely accepted reference points.

In this environment, people begin to assemble their own working rules for truth. These rules are rarely written down or consciously articulated. They develop through experience, emotion, and repeated exposure to certain kinds of explanations. Over time, a person comes to recognize which stories feel plausible, which voices feel trustworthy, and which claims trigger immediate skepticism.

These personal rules often rely less on formal evidence and more on pattern recognition. People notice what seems to line up with their experiences and what feels out of sync. They pay attention to whether a story resonates emotionally, whether it fits with what people like them are saying, and whether it seems to explain confusing events in a way that feels coherent.

Trust becomes tied to familiarity and alignment. A source that uses familiar language, expresses shared concerns, or reflects a person's values can feel more credible than a distant expert using technical terms. The sense that "this person understands people like me" becomes a powerful signal of trustworthiness.

Over time, these signals harden into expectations. People come to anticipate which sources will "tell it straight" and which ones will "spin things." These expectations guide attention before any specific claim is evaluated. A story from a favored source may be accepted quickly. A story from a disfavored source may be dismissed before it is fully considered.

This process feels intuitive rather than deliberate. People experience it as common sense. They say things like, "You can just tell when something isn't right," or "That doesn't pass the smell test." These reactions are not random. They reflect internalized rules that have developed over time about what counts as believable.

Emotion plays a larger role in these judgments than most people realize. If a story reduces anxiety, confirms a sense of understanding, or provides moral clarity, it often feels more true. If a story increases uncertainty, threatens identity, or creates discomfort, it often feels suspect. The feeling of truth becomes closely tied to emotional impact.

This does not mean people are lying to themselves. It means that the mind is doing what it has always done: integrating feeling, experience, and social context into judgments about reality. In the absence of strong shared standards, this integration becomes more visible and more influential.

Social feedback further shapes these private standards. When a person's interpretations are affirmed by their community, those interpretations gain weight. Agreement does not just feel validating. It also reinforces the sense that one's way of deciding what is true is reasonable and shared. Disagreement, especially from outside the group, can feel less like a factual correction and more like a challenge to identity.

Over time, these private standards form a kind of internal compass. People may not be able to explain exactly why they trust some sources and not others, but they feel confident in their judgments. What began as adaptation becomes conviction. The personal system feels stable, even if it would look inconsistent from the outside.

This is one reason why debates across different groups often feel fruitless. The disagreement is not just about specific facts. It is about different internal standards for what counts as a fact in the first place. Each side is using a different set of rules to decide what is real.

When people talk past each other in this way, it can be tempting to assume bad faith or ignorance. More often, what is happening is that two different personal systems are colliding. Each system feels internally coherent to the person using it. Each feels like common sense.

Understanding this shift helps explain why appeals to evidence alone often fail. Evidence only matters if it is evaluated within a system that treats it as meaningful. When people operate with different internal standards, the same piece of information can be interpreted in completely different ways.

In a world where shared standards are weak, deciding what is true becomes a deeply personal process. People are not just choosing facts. They are choosing the rules by which facts are recognized. Those rules shape not only what they believe, but how they understand themselves and their place in the world.

# CHAPTER 6

Identity-Based Credibility

Identity-Based Credibility

## Identity-Based Credibility

When shared standards weaken, credibility does not disappear. It becomes more closely tied to identity. Who someone is begins to matter as much as, or more than, what they say. Trust shifts from being based primarily on role, training, or institutional position to being based on perceived belonging and alignment.

People increasingly ask, often without realizing it, whether a source feels like "one of us." Shared background, shared language, shared frustrations, and shared values become shortcuts for deciding whether someone is worth listening to. These cues feel personal and immediate. They can override more abstract signals of expertise.

This does not require explicit tribalism. It can operate quietly. A person may feel more comfortable trusting someone who seems to live a similar life, face similar pressures, or express familiar concerns. That comfort can translate into credibility. The source feels real in a way that distant institutions do not.

Identity-based credibility is reinforced by storytelling. People are more likely to trust narratives that reflect their own experiences or the experiences of people they identify with. A story told by someone who seems to share your world can feel more true than statistics delivered by someone who feels removed from it.

Over time, these patterns create credibility bubbles. Within a given group, certain voices rise to prominence because they speak in ways that resonate with group identity. Those voices become interpreters of reality for the group. Their framing of events shapes how members understand what is happening and what it means.

Challenges to those voices are often experienced as challenges to the group itself. If someone questions a trusted insider, it can feel less like a factual disagreement and more like an attack on shared identity. Defending the source becomes a way of defending the group and one's place within it.

This dynamic helps explain why debates across identity lines often escalate quickly. People are not just defending claims. They are defending relationships and belonging. A disagreement about facts becomes tangled with questions of loyalty, respect, and recognition.

From the outside, identity-based credibility can look irrational. From the inside, it feels protective. It helps people avoid sources that have historically dismissed, misunderstood, or spoken down to them. Trusting insiders can feel like an act of self-respect.

At the same time, this shift narrows the range of voices that feel acceptable. If credibility is tied closely to identity, then outsiders face a high barrier to being heard, even when they have relevant expertise. What matters is not only what they know, but whether they are perceived as part of the right world to belong to.

As identity-based credibility becomes more central, reality itself becomes more group-specific. Different communities develop different trusted narrators. Those narrators emphasize different threats, different priorities, and different explanations. Shared reality becomes harder to maintain, even when people are exposed to similar information.

This does not mean that people are choosing identity over truth in a conscious way. It means that identity becomes part of how truth is recognized. The question "Is this true?" becomes intertwined with the question "Who is saying this, and do they understand people like me?"

Once this pattern is established, it is self-reinforcing. The more a group relies on its own trusted voices, the less practice it has evaluating claims from outside. Over time, outside perspectives can feel not just wrong, but irrelevant or suspect by default.

Identity-based credibility fills an important gap left by weakened institutions. It offers people a way to feel seen and understood. It provides a sense of common interpretation. It also fragments the broader landscape of trust, making it harder to find common ground.

In a trust vacuum, identity becomes a powerful organizing principle. It does not replace the need for truth. It reshapes how truth is located, recognized, and defended. Credibility becomes something you belong to, not just something you earn.

# CHAPTER 7
# Subcultures As Trust Infrastructure

## Subcultures As Trust Infrastructure

As institutional authority weakens and identity-based credibility grows, subcultures take on a larger role in organizing trust. These are not just hobby groups or casual communities. They become places where shared interpretations are built, tested, and reinforced. Within these spaces, people develop common ways of talking about what is happening and why it matters.

Subcultures provide more than social connection. They offer reality scaffolding. Members learn which sources are acceptable, which explanations are taken seriously, and which narratives are considered obvious or suspect. Over time, these shared expectations create a local sense of what counts as common sense.

Participation in a subculture often brings relief. Instead of navigating uncertainty alone, people enter a space where others already share similar concerns and interpretations. Confusing events feel more manageable when they are quickly fitted into a familiar framework. The group supplies not only answers, but a way of recognizing which questions matter.

Language plays an important role in this process. Subcultures develop their own terms, shorthand, and reference points. These shared linguistic cues help members signal belonging and quickly align on meaning. Once people speak the same way about events, it becomes easier to feel that they also see the same reality.

Subcultures also provide emotional regulation. Shared reactions help members calibrate how worried, angry, or hopeful they should feel. If the group treats an event as alarming, members are more likely to experience it that way. If the group treats something as overblown, members may downplay it as well. Emotional tone becomes part of how the group interprets reality.

Over time, subcultures can become closed loops. Information that fits the group's narrative is circulated and reinforced. Information that challenges it may be ignored, reinterpreted, or treated as hostile. This does not usually happen through explicit censorship. It happens through patterns of attention, validation, and social reward.

Belonging strengthens these dynamics. When people feel accepted and understood within a group, they are more likely to adopt the group's interpretations. Agreement becomes a way of maintaining connection. Disagreement can feel risky, even when doubts are present.

From the outside, this can look like echo chambers. From the inside, it often feels like finally finding people who see things clearly. The sense of shared insight can be powerful. It reinforces the feeling that the group has access to truths that others are missing.

Subcultures also compete with each other. Different groups offer different explanations for the same events. Each presents its own version of what is really going on. As more people rely on subcultural frameworks, the broader public sphere fragments into overlapping but incompatible interpretations.

This fragmentation makes cross-group communication harder. When people from different subcultures talk, they may use the same words but mean different things. They may interpret the same evidence in different ways. Conversations can become tense, not because people are unwilling to listen, but because they are operating from different interpretive baselines.

Subcultures fill an important psychological need. They provide belonging, shared meaning, and a sense of orientation. They also create boundaries around trust. Who you listen to and what you believe are shaped by which group you feel part of.

In a trust vacuum, subcultures become informal institutions. They take on roles that formal structures once played. They organize credibility, supply narratives, and offer emotional and social reinforcement. They are not just communities of interest. They are communities of interpretation.

As these communities grow in influence, they become central to how people experience reality. What feels obvious, questionable, or urgent is increasingly determined by subcultural membership. Trust is no longer primarily national, professional, or institutional. It becomes local, relational, and group-based.

# CHAPTER 8

## Influencers, Para-Experts, and Private Authorities

## Influencers, Para-Experts, and Private Authorities

As subcultures grow more central to how people organize trust, certain individuals within those spaces rise to positions of influence. These are not always formal leaders. They are often people who speak confidently, interpret events in ways that resonate, and provide a steady stream of explanations. Over time, they become reference points for how others in the group understand what is happening.

These figures occupy a space between expert and peer. They may not have traditional credentials, but they present themselves as knowledgeable, experienced, or uniquely informed. Their authority comes from perceived insight, consistency, and alignment with the group's worldview. Listeners or followers begin to treat their interpretations as guides for how to think about unfolding events.

Para-experts often position themselves as translators. They claim to break down complex topics in ways that "regular people" can understand. This can make their explanations feel more accessible and more honest than institutional messaging. The sense that someone is cutting through jargon and telling it straight carries strong appeal.

Private authorities also benefit from narrative continuity. Institutions tend to speak in fragments, through press releases, changing spokespeople, and formal updates. Influencers and para-experts, by contrast, offer an ongoing story. They connect new events to previous claims, creating a sense of coherence over time. This narrative thread can make their worldview feel internally consistent, even when specific details change.

Relational trust deepens this effect. Followers hear these voices regularly. They learn the speaker's style, values, and emotional rhythms. Over time, the voice itself becomes familiar. Familiarity can be mistaken for reliability. The person feels known, even though the relationship is one-sided.

These figures also provide emotional framing. They model how to react. They show when to be outraged, when to be skeptical, when to feel vindicated, and when to feel threatened. This emotional guidance becomes part of their authority. People do not just look to them for information. They look to them for cues about how to feel.

Challenges to these private authorities are often experienced as personal attacks by followers. If someone questions the influencer's claims, it can feel like questioning the group's shared reality. Loyalty becomes entangled with belief. Defending the figure becomes a way of defending one's own interpretive framework.

From the outside, this can look like people elevating unqualified voices. From the inside, it feels like listening to someone who understands the situation better than distant institutions do. The para-expert's strength is not formal expertise at all. It is perceived attunement to the group's concerns and experiences.

Over time, private authorities can accumulate significant power. They shape what topics are discussed, which interpretations gain traction, and which explanations are dismissed. Their influence can rival or exceed that of traditional institutions within certain communities.

This does not mean that these figures are always wrong or malicious. Many are responding to real gaps in communication and trust. They step into spaces where institutions have failed to persuade, explain, or listen. The issue is not their existence. It is the weight they come to carry in defining reality.

As more people rely on these private authorities, the center of gravity for credibility shifts further away from shared standards. Reality becomes increasingly mediated by individual voices and personalized narratives. What counts as true depends more on who you follow than on any common process for evaluation.

In a trust vacuum, influencers and para-experts become more than content creators. They become architects of meaning. They help build the frameworks through which people interpret the world. Their reach is not just informational. It is psychological and social. They are not simply talking about reality. They are helping to construct it.

# CHAPTER 9

# The Moral Authority of "Do Your Own Research?

THE MORAL AUTHORITY OF "DO YOUR OWN RESEARCH"

# The Moral Authority of "Do Your Own Research"

The phrase "do your own research" once described a method. It meant checking sources, comparing evidence, and not relying on a single authority. Over time, it has taken on a different function. It has become a moral stance, a way of signaling independence, dignity, and resistance to imposed authority.

In a trust vacuum, this shift makes sense. When institutions no longer feel reliable, people look for ways to assert control over how they form beliefs. Saying "do your own research" communicates that a person is not passively accepting what they are told. It frames belief as something earned through personal effort rather than received from above.

The phrase also carries social meaning. It separates people who see themselves as independent thinkers from those they view as unquestioning followers. This distinction is not just about information. It is about identity. To say "I did my own research" is to say something about who you are and how you relate to power.

Over time, the method and the identity become intertwined. Research is no longer just an activity. It becomes proof of moral standing. The act of questioning authority is treated as inherently virtuous, regardless of the quality of the sources or the rigor of the process.

This creates a paradox. The more "do your own research" functions as a moral badge, the harder it becomes to question how that research is actually done. Critiquing someone's sources or methods can be experienced as a personal attack. It feels like challenging their independence rather than evaluating their claims.

Within subcultures, "doing your own research" often follows predictable paths. People are pointed toward particular websites, videos, or personalities. Over time, these become the accepted research channels within the group. The posture remains individualistic, but the information flow becomes standardized.

This allows people to feel both independent and aligned. They experience themselves as free thinkers while drawing from a shared pool of interpretations. The moral language of independence masks the reality of coordinated belief formation.

The phrase also shifts responsibility. If everyone is supposed to do their own research, then failures of shared understanding can be framed as personal shortcomings. Disagreement becomes evidence that someone else has not done enough work, rather than a sign that people are operating with different standards or sources.

This framing makes dialogue more difficult. Instead of comparing evidence or reasoning, people end up comparing virtue. Who has really looked into it, and who is just repeating talking points. The debate moves from facts to character.

For many people, this stance feels empowering. It offers a sense of agency in a confusing environment. It allows people to feel that they are not being manipulated. That sense of empowerment is real, even when the underlying information channels are narrow or biased.

The moral authority of "do your own research" fills a gap left by weakened institutions. It provides a way to assert personal credibility when institutional credibility is in doubt. It becomes a substitute for shared processes of verification.

The result is not pure individualism. It is a new form of collective belief built on the language of independence. People are no longer told what to think. They are told to go discover the same conclusions for themselves.

In this way, "do your own research" becomes one of the central values of the trust vacuum. It signals self-respect, autonomy, and resistance. It also quietly reshapes how truth is recognized, defended, and debated.

# CHAPTER 10
# Narrative Authority vs. Institutional Authority

## Narrative Authority vs. Institutional Authority

As institutional authority weakens, stories take on greater power. Lived experience, personal testimony, and narrative coherence begin to feel more convincing than formal data or expert consensus. This is not because people have stopped caring about evidence. It is because stories answer questions that statistics often do not.

Narratives offer meaning, not just information. They connect events into a sequence that feels understandable. They assign motives, causes, and consequences in ways that help people make sense of complexity. A good story explains not only what happened, but why it matters and how it fits into a larger picture.

Institutional communication tends to fragment experience. It separates facts into reports, updates, and technical categories. This can be accurate, but it often feels emotionally thin. It does not always help people understand how new information connects to their own lives or to broader patterns they think they see.

Personal narratives fill that gap. A single story can feel more real than a large dataset. Hearing how something affected one person can carry more emotional weight than hearing how it affected ten thousand. This is not a failure of logic. It is how human attention and empathy work.

Narrative authority also feels more flexible. Stories can adapt quickly. They can incorporate new events without waiting for formal review. They can explain contradictions by reframing them as part of a larger plot. This adaptability can make narrative systems feel more responsive than institutional ones.

Once people rely on narrative authority, they often judge claims based on whether they fit the story they already accept. New information is evaluated for how well it integrates into the existing narrative arc. If it fits, it feels credible. If it disrupts the story, it feels suspicious or forced.

This creates a powerful filter for belief. People may accept weak evidence if it supports a compelling narrative. They may reject strong evidence if it threatens the coherence of the story they rely on. The narrative becomes the primary organizing structure for belief.

From the outside, this can look like people choosing anecdotes over data. From the inside, it feels like choosing explanations that make sense of lived experience over abstract numbers that feel disconnected from reality.

Narrative authority also personalizes trust. People trust storytellers they relate to. They trust voices that reflect their concerns, fears, and hopes. The storyteller becomes part of the narrative. Their credibility is tied to their perceived authenticity, not to external validation.

Institutional authority, by contrast, depends on procedures, credentials, and standardized methods. These can feel distant and impersonal. When trust in those systems weakens, their outputs lose persuasive force, even when they are accurate.

Over time, narrative authority can become self-sealing. The story explains why institutions cannot be trusted. Institutional corrections are then interpreted as part of the story itself. What begins as a narrative becomes a closed interpretive loop.

This does not mean narratives are inherently deceptive. Humans have always relied on stories to understand the world. The shift described here is about relative weight. Stories move from being one way of understanding to being the primary way of deciding what is real.

In a trust vacuum, narrative authority often outperforms institutional authority. It feels more human, more responsive, and more connected to everyday experience. The result is not the disappearance of facts, but the dominance of stories in organizing how facts are interpreted.

# CHAPTER 11
# Conspiracy As Coherent Reality-Building

## Conspiracy As Coherent Reality-Building

Conspiracy thinking is often treated as a failure of reasoning. From that perspective, it looks like people accepting implausible explanations or ignoring obvious evidence. That framing misses what conspiracy systems actually provide. For many people, conspiratorial narratives offer a way to restore coherence in a world that feels confusing, contradictory, or hostile.

Conspiracies supply structure. They turn scattered events into a connected story. Instead of randomness or institutional incompetence, they offer intentional actors, hidden causes, and clear lines of responsibility. This can feel more satisfying than explanations that emphasize uncertainty, complexity, or systemic failure.

These narratives also provide moral clarity. They identify villains and victims. They sort the world into those who are awake and those who are deceived. This framing reduces ambiguity. It tells people who to trust, who to blame, and where to place their anger or fear. In environments of low institutional trust, that clarity can feel stabilizing.

Conspiracy systems often position themselves as uncovering hidden truth. The believer is not just informed. They are initiated. They see what others cannot or will not see. This creates a sense of special knowledge and personal significance. It transforms confusion into insight and powerlessness into understanding.

Conspiracy narratives are rarely isolated claims. They are full interpretive frameworks. Once adopted, they become lenses through which new information is filtered. Events are not evaluated on their own terms. They are interpreted for how they fit into the larger story.

This makes these narratives resistant to disconfirmation. Evidence that contradicts the narrative can be reinterpreted as part of the cover-up. Institutional corrections can be seen as proof that powerful actors are trying to suppress the truth. The system contains built-in explanations for why it cannot be easily challenged.

From the outside, this can look like stubbornness or bad faith. From the inside, it feels like consistency. The narrative explains why dissenting information is unreliable. What looks like closed-mindedness to others feels like vigilance to the believer.

Conspiracy frameworks also provide community. People who share the same narrative recognize each other as part of an in-group. They exchange interpretations, reinforce each other's conclusions, and validate each other's suspicions. This social reinforcement strengthens the system and makes it harder to abandon.

These systems can be emotionally regulating. They give people somewhere to place fear, anger, and uncertainty. Instead of diffuse anxiety, there is a focused explanation. Instead of helplessness, there is a sense of opposition and purpose. The narrative offers a way to organize emotional experience as well as belief.

It is important to note that conspiracy thinking does not usually begin with extreme or fantastical claims. It often starts with real distrust, real grievances, or real experiences of being misled. The narrative grows as people look for explanations that match the level of emotional intensity they feel.

In this sense, conspiracy systems function as replacement realities. They do not just answer specific questions. They provide a complete way of interpreting the world. They tell people what matters, who is credible, and how to read events. They fill many of the same psychological roles that institutions once filled.

Understanding conspiracy thinking in this way does not require endorsing the claims. It requires recognizing the function. These narratives persist not only because of misinformation, but because they offer coherence, identity, and emotional organization in environments where shared standards have weakened.

In a trust vacuum, conspiracy systems are not anomalies. They are one of the most complete forms of replacement reality. They show, in a concentrated way, what many other informal credibility systems are doing more quietly. They are attempts to rebuild a world that makes sense when the old one no longer does.

# CHAPTER 12

# Why Conspiracies Persist After Disconfirmation

# Why Conspiracies Persist After Disconfirmation

When people outside a conspiracy framework present contradictory evidence, they often expect the belief to weaken or collapse. From a purely factual standpoint, that expectation makes sense. If a claim is shown to be false, it should lose its force. In practice, conspiracy systems often survive repeated disconfirmation with little visible damage.

This persistence is not primarily about ignorance. It is about how the narrative is structured and what it is doing for the person who holds it. Once a conspiracy framework is in place, it becomes more than a set of claims. It becomes a way of organizing experience.

Disconfirming evidence is rarely evaluated in isolation. It is interpreted through the lens of the larger story. If the narrative already assumes that institutions, media, or experts are deceptive, then corrections from those sources are not neutral. They are treated as expected moves within the plot. The very act of correction can be taken as confirmation that something is being hidden.

Conspiracy systems also include explanations for why evidence might look convincing while still being false. Concepts like planted stories, compromised experts, and manufactured consensus allow believers to absorb contradictory information without abandoning the core narrative. The system does not break. It expands.

There is also a social cost to disconfirmation. Accepting that a conspiracy narrative is wrong can mean losing connection with a community that has provided understanding, belonging, and shared identity. It can mean admitting that time, emotion, and trust were invested in something that no longer holds. For many people, that loss feels heavier than the cost of maintaining the belief.

Emotion plays a central role. Conspiracy narratives often carry strong feelings of anger, fear, and moral certainty. These emotions are not easily set aside just because a factual claim is challenged. Letting go of the story can feel like letting go of the emotional framework that has helped make sense of distressing experiences.

## Why Conspiracies Persist After Disconfirmation

In some cases, disconfirmation can even strengthen commitment. When a believer feels attacked or ridiculed, they may double down as a way of defending dignity and autonomy. Holding onto the belief becomes a form of resistance. It signals independence and loyalty to the group.

There is also the problem of partial fit. Even when specific predictions fail, parts of the narrative may still seem to explain other events. The believer does not evaluate the system as a whole. They focus on the pieces that still feel relevant. The story remains usable, even if some details are quietly dropped or reinterpreted.

Over time, conspiracy systems become flexible. They shift emphasis. They absorb new claims. They quietly retire old ones. This adaptability allows the framework to survive without ever fully confronting its own failures. The story evolves, but the core assumptions remain intact.

From the outside, this can look like moving the goalposts. From the inside, it feels like updating the story as new information emerges. The believer experiences continuity, not contradiction.

What makes this especially powerful is that conspiracy systems position themselves as fundamentally opposed to official reality. If official reality says the conspiracy is false, that can be taken as exactly what the conspiracy would predict. Disconfirmation becomes part of the narrative logic rather than a challenge to it.

This does not mean that people are incapable of changing their minds. Many do. But change usually comes through shifts in identity, relationships, and emotional needs, not through isolated factual corrections. When the psychological function of the narrative is no longer needed, the belief may loosen. When it is still doing important work, it is likely to persist.

Understanding this persistence helps explain why debates framed purely around facts so often fail. The disagreement is not just about what is true. It is about what the story is doing for the person's sense of order, belonging, and meaning.

In a trust vacuum, conspiracy narratives survive not because they are airtight, but because they are useful. They provide a structure that helps people live with uncertainty, anger, and distrust. As long as that structure is needed, disconfirmation alone is unlikely to dismantle it.

# CHAPTER 13
# Competing Realities and Social Friction

## Competing Realities and Social Friction

When different groups operate with different frameworks for deciding what is real, everyday interactions become more strained. Disagreements are no longer just about opinions or interpretations. They are about the underlying rules for how reality itself is defined. This makes conflict more personal and more difficult to resolve.

In earlier periods, people could often assume that they were arguing within a shared structure. Even if they disagreed strongly, they usually accepted the same basic standards for evidence, authority, and legitimacy. That shared ground made compromise and mutual understanding possible, even when emotions ran high.

As replacement systems take hold, that shared ground weakens. People may use the same words but mean different things. They may refer to the same events but interpret them through entirely different narratives. What looks like disagreement on the surface is often disagreement at a deeper level about which reality system applies.

This creates a sense of talking past one another. Each side feels that the other is ignoring obvious facts or acting in bad faith. From each person's perspective, their own position feels grounded and reasonable. The other position feels distorted or dishonest.

Social friction increases as a result. Conversations that once felt manageable become tense. Family gatherings, workplaces, and community spaces become sites of conflict. People learn which topics to avoid and which relationships feel too strained to maintain.

Over time, people may begin to self-sort. They spend more time with those who share their framework and less time with those who do not. This reduces exposure to alternative interpretations. It also increases confidence that one's own way of seeing things is normal and widely shared.

This self-sorting reinforces polarization, but it is not only ideological. People are clustering around different rules for what counts as real. Each cluster becomes its own small reality with its own trusted sources and internal logic.

Attempts to bridge these divides often fail because they target surface disagreements rather than underlying frameworks. Presenting more facts does little if the two sides do not agree on how facts should be evaluated. Appeals to shared values fall flat if people no longer agree on which authorities define those values.

This kind of friction is exhausting. It creates a sense that social life requires constant vigilance. People may feel that they are always one conversation away from conflict. This can lead to withdrawal, cynicism, or a narrowing of social worlds.

From the outside, it can look like people are becoming more intolerant. From the inside, it often feels like self-protection. Avoiding certain conversations or relationships becomes a way to preserve emotional stability.

The loss of shared reality also affects institutions and organizations. Workplaces struggle with internal trust. Schools navigate conflicting expectations. Public discourse becomes fragmented. Coordination becomes harder when people cannot agree on basic descriptions of what is happening.

This fragmentation does not mean people no longer want social cohesion. Most people still value connection and understanding. The problem is that connection now requires navigating incompatible reality systems. That task is emotionally and cognitively demanding.

In a trust vacuum, social friction is not a side effect. It is a central feature. When people build different replacement systems for reality, those systems inevitably collide. The result is a social environment where disagreement feels deeper, more personal, and harder to repair.

Understanding this dynamic helps explain why so many people report feeling that something has changed in everyday interactions. It is not just that people disagree more. It is that they disagree from different realities. The friction is not only about opinions. It is about whose version of the world is being treated as real.

# CHAPTER 14

# The Psychological Costs and Benefits of Replacement Systems

# The Psychological Costs and Benefits of Replacement Systems

Replacement systems do not spread only because they are persuasive. They spread because they do real psychological work for the people who adopt them. In a world where shared authority has weakened, these systems offer stability, meaning, and a sense of orientation. They help people function in environments that would otherwise feel unmanageable.

One of the main benefits is reduced uncertainty. A replacement system provides ready-made explanations for confusing events. It supplies a framework for interpreting news, personal experiences, and social conflict. This reduces the need to constantly reevaluate everything from scratch. Life feels more predictable when events can be quickly placed into a familiar story.

These systems also support identity. They offer ways of understanding who you are and where you belong. They tell you what kinds of people are trustworthy, what kinds of people are suspect, and what values define your group. This identity support can be deeply comforting, especially when older sources of identity feel unstable or discredited.

Belonging is another major benefit. Replacement systems often come with communities, whether formal or informal. These communities provide validation, shared language, and emotional reinforcement. Feeling part of a group that "gets it" can counter isolation and help people feel less alone in a confusing world.

Replacement systems also simplify moral life. They clarify who is right and who is wrong. They reduce gray areas. This can be psychologically relieving. Moral complexity is tiring. Having a clear framework for assigning blame, responsibility, and virtue makes emotional life feel more manageable.

At the same time, these benefits come with real costs. Replacement systems narrow perception. Once a framework is adopted, it shapes what is noticed and what is ignored. Information that fits the system is amplified. Information that challenges it is downplayed or rejected. Over time, this can limit exposure to alternative explanations and reduce flexibility in thinking.

These systems can also increase conflict. When different groups operate with different replacement frameworks, disagreements become harder to resolve. Each system feels internally coherent. Each group experiences the other as misinformed or dishonest. The psychological stability of one group becomes the social friction of the larger community.

There is also an emotional cost. Replacement systems often rely on sustained levels of anger, fear, or vigilance. Maintaining a narrative that emphasizes threat or deception can keep people in a heightened emotional state. This can contribute to stress, exhaustion, and a sense that the world is hostile.

Dependency is another risk. As people rely more heavily on a replacement system to organize reality, their ability to tolerate uncertainty on their own can weaken. The system becomes a psychological crutch. Without it, people may feel disoriented or anxious. This makes it harder to step back or reconsider the framework, even when doubts arise.

Replacement systems can also become more rigid over time. What begins as a flexible way of making sense of confusion can harden into fixed doctrine. The system becomes something that must be defended rather than examined. Questioning it can feel like a threat to identity, belonging, and emotional stability.

From the inside, these costs are often invisible. The system feels like protection. It feels like clarity. It feels like truth. The narrowing of perception and the emotional strain are experienced as necessary responses to a dangerous or deceptive world.

From the outside, the costs can be easier to see. Relationships strain. Dialogue becomes harder. People seem less open to new information. The social environment becomes more brittle.

Understanding both the benefits and the costs is essential. Replacement systems are not simply errors to be corrected. They are adaptations to real psychological pressures. They help people cope with a loss of shared authority. They also create new forms of rigidity, conflict, and emotional burden.

## The Trust Vacuum

In a trust vacuum, replacement systems are both stabilizers and stressors. They allow people to function in a fragmented reality. They also deepen fragmentation over time. The same systems that make life feel more manageable for individuals can make shared reality harder to sustain.

WHAT SHARED REALITY USED TO DO

# CHAPTER 15
# What Shared Reality Used To Do

## What Shared Reality Used To Do

## What Shared Reality Used To Do

It can be difficult to remember how much psychological work shared reality once carried. When institutions were more widely trusted, they did more than provide information or services. They created a common reference point that allowed people to coordinate their understanding of the world, even when they disagreed about specific conclusions.

Shared reality reduced the burden on individuals. People did not have to build their own full systems for deciding what was real. They could rely on a set of commonly accepted standards for evidence, expertise, and legitimacy. This did not guarantee accuracy, but it provided a stable backdrop for everyday decision-making.

One of the key functions of shared reality was conflict containment. Disagreements could be intense, but they usually occurred within a shared frame. People argued about what should be done, not about whether basic descriptions of events were valid. This made it easier to compromise, to accept losses, and to continue working together after disputes.

Shared reality also supported trust in processes, even when trust in outcomes was limited. A person might believe that a particular decision was wrong while still believing that it was reached through a legitimate process. That distinction mattered. It allowed people to stay engaged without feeling that the entire system was corrupt or meaningless.

Another function was emotional regulation at a social level. When people could assume that others were seeing roughly the same world, they could calibrate their reactions. If everyone treated something as a minor issue, it was easier to downshift concern. If everyone treated something as serious, it was easier to mobilize collective attention. Shared reality helped pace collective emotion.

It also supported social trust. People could interact with strangers, coworkers, and institutions with a baseline expectation of shared assumptions. That reduced friction. It made coordination possible without constant negotiation over what was real, who was credible, and which rules applied.

That shared framework gave people a sense of continuity. Even as specific leaders, policies, or narratives changed, the underlying framework felt stable. This made change feel less threatening. People could adapt to new information without feeling that the ground itself was constantly shifting.

Shared reality did not require universal agreement. It required shared standards. People could disagree passionately while still accepting the same basic rules for how disagreements were settled. That distinction allowed pluralism to function without collapsing into fragmentation.

As shared reality weakened, many of these functions became harder to sustain. Individuals took on more of the work that institutions once performed. Conflict became more personal. Emotional regulation became more fragmented. Trust in processes eroded along with trust in outcomes.

Looking back, it can be tempting to idealize the past. Shared reality was never perfect. Institutions made mistakes. Voices were excluded. Power was unevenly distributed. But even with those flaws, shared reality performed important psychological and social labor.

Understanding what shared reality used to do helps clarify what has been lost. It also helps explain why replacement systems feel so compelling. They are not just offering alternative beliefs. They are trying to perform functions that were once carried by widely trusted structures.

In a trust vacuum, people are not only looking for answers. They are looking for the scaffolding that makes answers usable in everyday life. Shared reality once provided that scaffolding. Its weakening leaves a gap that no single replacement system can fully fill.

# CHAPTER 16
Reality After Institutions

## Reality After Institutions

## Reality After Institutions

Living after institutions does not mean living without institutions. It means living in a world where no single institution reliably organizes reality for everyone. Authority still exists, but it is distributed, contested, and filtered through informal systems. The result is not the absence of structure, but a landscape of overlapping structures that compete to define what is real.

In this environment, people are required to do more interpretive work. They must constantly decide which sources to trust, which narratives to adopt, and which communities to align with. The burden of reality construction shifts from shared frameworks to individuals and small groups. This makes everyday life more cognitively and emotionally demanding.

Some people respond by narrowing their worlds. They reduce exposure to conflicting interpretations. They lean more heavily on trusted voices and familiar narratives. This can provide a sense of stability, but it also increases isolation from alternative perspectives. The world becomes smaller, even as information becomes more abundant.

Others respond by becoming perpetual interpreters. They constantly cross-check, compare, and reassess. This can feel responsible and open-minded. It can also become exhausting. Without shared anchors, the work of interpretation never really ends.

Over time, these different strategies shape different kinds of psychological lives. Some people experience a tightening of reality around a single framework. Others experience a chronic sense of instability. Both are ways of coping with a world where shared standards are weak.

What emerges is not a clean replacement for institutional reality. It is a patchwork. Different people live in different interpretive worlds. They share physical space, but not always the same sense of what is happening or why. Coordination becomes harder. Misunderstanding becomes more common.

This does not mean that a return to past forms of institutional authority is likely or even desirable. Many institutions lost trust for real reasons. The point is not to romanticize what was. The point is to recognize the psychological and social work that institutions once did and to understand what happens when that work is no longer widely shared.

Living after institutions requires new skills. People need greater tolerance for uncertainty. They need ways to engage with disagreement without assuming bad faith. They need to recognize how their own interpretive systems shape what feels obvious or true. Without that awareness, fragmentation becomes self-reinforcing.

It also requires new forms of humility. In a fragmented reality, confidence is easy to come by. Certainty is rewarded within small groups. What is harder is holding the possibility that one's own framework is partial, shaped by identity, community, and emotional needs as much as by evidence.

None of this offers a simple solution. The trust vacuum is not something that can be filled once and for all. It is a condition of the current environment. People will continue to build replacement systems. Some will be more flexible than others. Some will allow for shared space. Others will harden into closed worlds.

The future of shared reality is not predetermined. It will depend on whether new forms of coordination, credibility, and mutual recognition can emerge. It will depend on whether people can rebuild not just trust in specific institutions, but trust in common processes for deciding what is real.

This book has not argued that people are irrational for building their own systems. It has argued that they are responding to real psychological pressures. When shared authority weakens, people do what humans have always done. They create meaning structures that allow them to function.

Reality after institutions is not empty. It is crowded. It is shaped by stories, relationships, identities, and informal authorities. Understanding this does not solve the problem. It does, however, make the problem visible.

In a world where no single voice reliably defines reality, the task is not to eliminate replacement systems. The task is to understand them, to see the psychological work they are doing, and to recognize both their limits and their appeal.

Living after institutions means living with that tension. It means navigating a world where reality is built as much as it is received. The question is not whether people will construct meaning. The question is whether those constructions can leave room for shared life in a fragmented world.

REALITY AFTER INSTITUTIONS

# THE END

www.ingramcontent.com/pod-product-compliance
Lightning Source LLC
Chambersburg PA
CBHW070646030426
42337CB00020B/4184